BASIC SKILLS SERIES

PROBABILITY
STATISTICS & GRAPHING

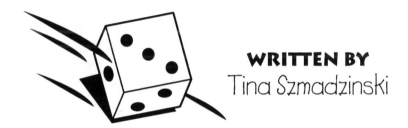

WRITTEN BY
Tina Szmadzinski

INSIDE ILLUSTRATIONS BY
Don Ellens

COVER ILLUSTRATION BY
Annette Hollister-Papp

Publisher
Instructional Fair • TS Denison
Grand Rapids, Michigan 49544

TABLE OF CONTENTS

Credits

Author: Tina Szmadzinski
Illustrations: Don Ellens
Cover Art: Annette Hollister-Papp
Project Director/Editor: Rhonda DeWaard
Editors: Alyson Kieda & Sharon Kirkwood
Production: Pat Geasler

About the Author

Tina Szmadzinski is an elementary teacher in Grand Rapids, Michigan, with over 17 years of classroom experience. She received her undergraduate degree from the University of Michigan. Tina's school involvement includes writing/developing math objectives, working on technology teams, and setting up cross-grade level tutoring and math clubs. She is also a math consultant for other school districts. Tina has written other books for Instructional Fair • TS Denison.

Permission to Reproduce

Standard Book Number: 1-56822-470-2
Probability, Statistics, & Graphing–Primary
Copyright © 1997 by Instructional Fair • TS Denison
2400 Turner Avenue NW
Grand Rapids, Michigan 49544
All Rights Reserved • Printed in the USA

Name _____

Use with page 4.

CLASS CLOTHES – DAY 1

Look around to see what your classmates are wearing today. Are they wearing jeans, other pants, dresses, or skirts? Make predictions about what you think they will wear tomorrow. Write a number inside each article of clothing showing your prediction.

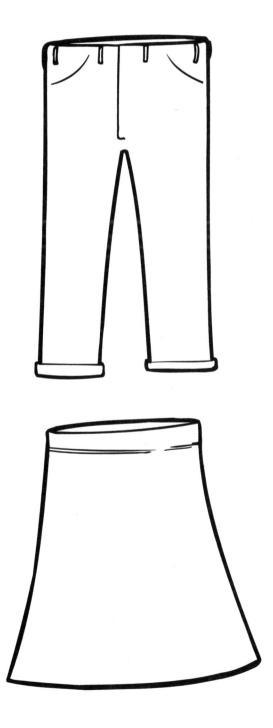

Name _____

Use with page 3.

CLASS CLOTHES – DAY 2

Count the number of students wearing each type of clothing. Color in that same number of circles in the correct column. Compare these numbers with the predictions you made yesterday.

Clothes Our Class Wore Today

Jeans	Other Pants	Dresses	Skirts
12	12	12	12
11	11	11	11
10	10	10	10
9	9	9	9
8	8	8	8
7	7	7	7
6	6	6	6
5	5	5	5
4	4	4	4
3	3	3	3
2	2	2	2
1	1	1	1

Name _____

Use with page 6.

RED AND BLACK ANTS

There are five ants on this anthill. Some are red ants and some are black ants. Color to show how many you think are black ants. Color to show how many you think are red ants.

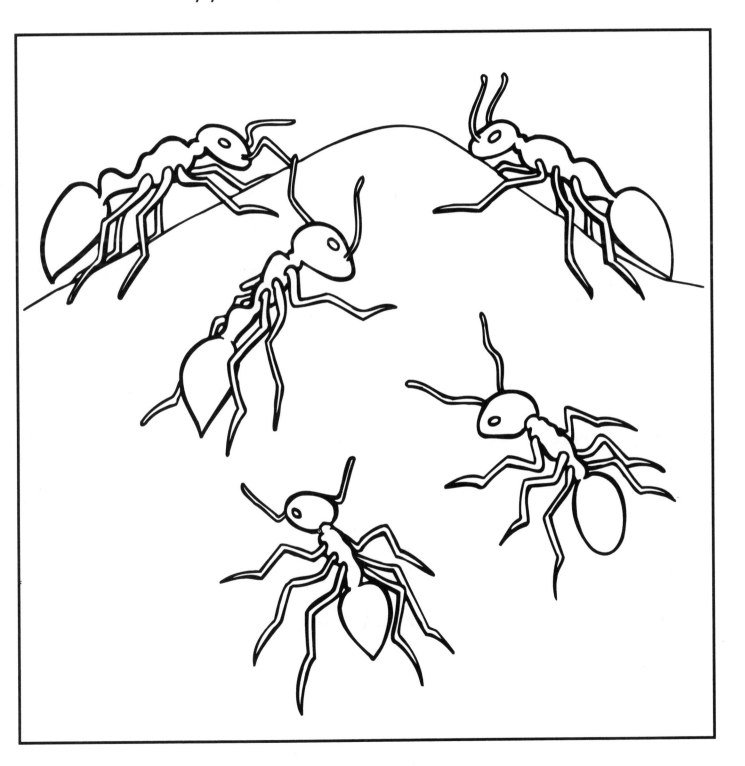

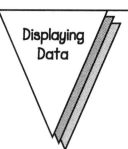
RED AND BLACK ANTS (CONTINUED)

Teacher Note: Cut out these headings and display on the left side of a bulletin board or floor graph. Have each student place his/her ant picture after the correct heading. Discuss the guesses that the students made.

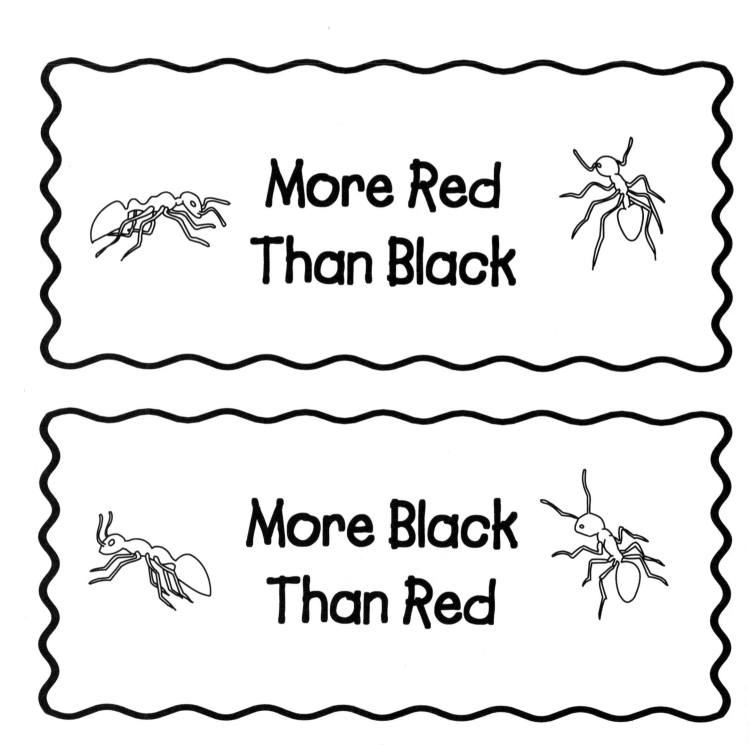

More Red
Than Black

More Black
Than Red

Name _____

Use with page 8.

POPPING POPCORN

Here are 10 popcorn kernels. Color how many you think will pop when they are heated.

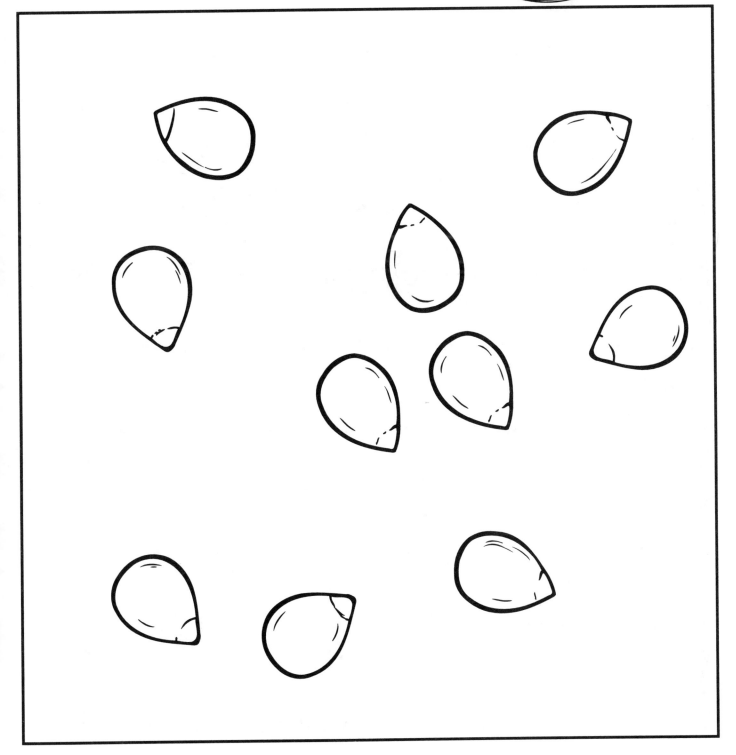

Use with page 7.

POPPING POPCORN (CONTINUED)

Teacher Note: Cut out these headings and display on the left side of a bulletin board or floor graph. Have each student place his/her popcorn picture after the correct heading. Discuss the guesses that the students made.

Five or More

Less Than Five

Name _____

PROBABILITY WITH BEADS

Color the square beads one color and the round beads another color. Then answer the questions below.

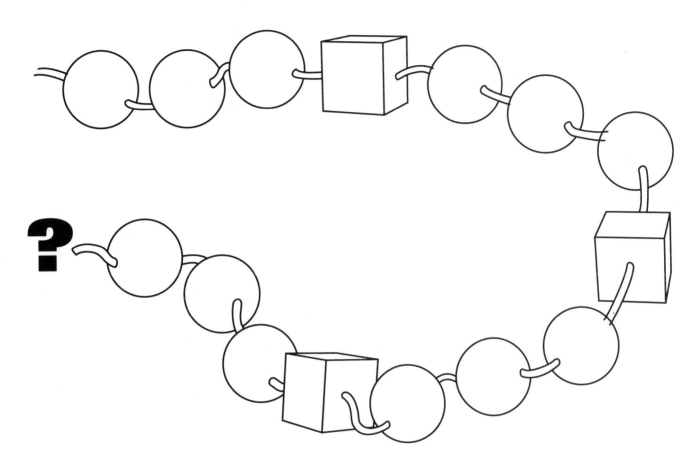

1. Look for the question mark (?) above. Which bead do you think should be in this spot? _____

   Why?_____

   _____

2. If the beads were mixed together in a bag and you reached in and pulled one out, which shape bead do you think it would be? _____Why?_____

   _____

Name _____

HEARTS AND DIAMONDS

Color the diamonds one color and the hearts a different color.
Then answer the questions below.

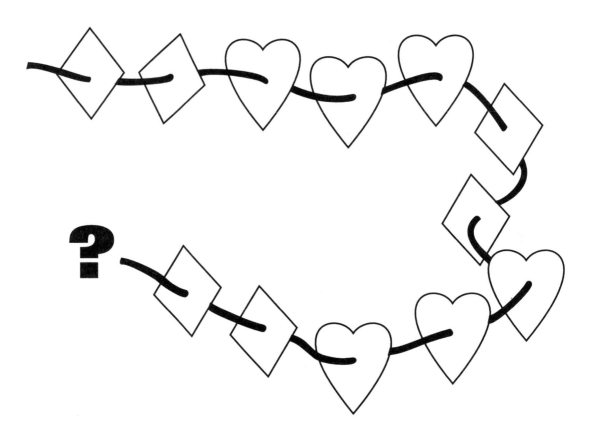

1. Look for the question mark (?) above. Which shape do you think

    should be in that spot? _____Why?_____

    _____

    _____

2. If the shapes were mixed together in a bag and you reached in and

    pulled one out, which shape do you think it would be?_____

    Why?_____

    _____

Name _____

JELLYBEAN JUMBLE

Use three different colors to color the jellybeans. Then answer the questions below.

1. If the jar spills, most of the jellybeans will be what color?

_____ Why?_____

2. If you reached in to take some jellybeans, what color would

most of them be ? _____ Why?_____

_____

Name _____

Use with page 13.

MY FAVORITE PET

Choose and color your favorite pet from the pictures below. Then cut your pet picture out and place it on the graph your teacher created on a bulletin board.

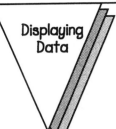
MY FAVORITE PET (CONTINUED)

Teacher Note: Cut out these headings and display on the left side of a bulletin board or floor graph. Have each student place his/her pet picture after the correct heading.

Rabbits

Cats

Fish

Dogs

Collecting Data

MUNCH AND CRUNCH

Talk with your class about their favorite snack foods. Ask each of your class-mates what his/her favorite snack foods are of those shown below and then record each response with a tally mark in the appropriate picture. Discuss how this data can be interpreted. Then complete page 15.

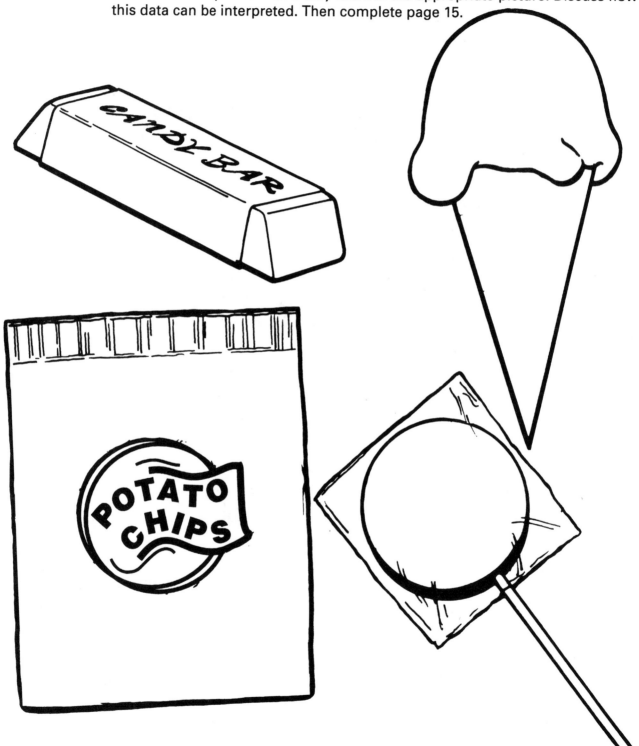

Extension Activity: The class might predict what another class would choose as their favorite snacks. After taking an actual survey, the results should be compared.

Name _____

Use with page 14.

MUNCH AND CRUNCH (CONTINUED)

Complete the following pictograph using the data recorded on the previous page.

Name _____

SUNNY SKIES

The pictures show the weather for one month. Look at the number of sunny, cloudy, and rainy days there were.

Create a pictograph using the data above.

Weather for One Month

Number of Days

YOUR BACKYARD

Name _____

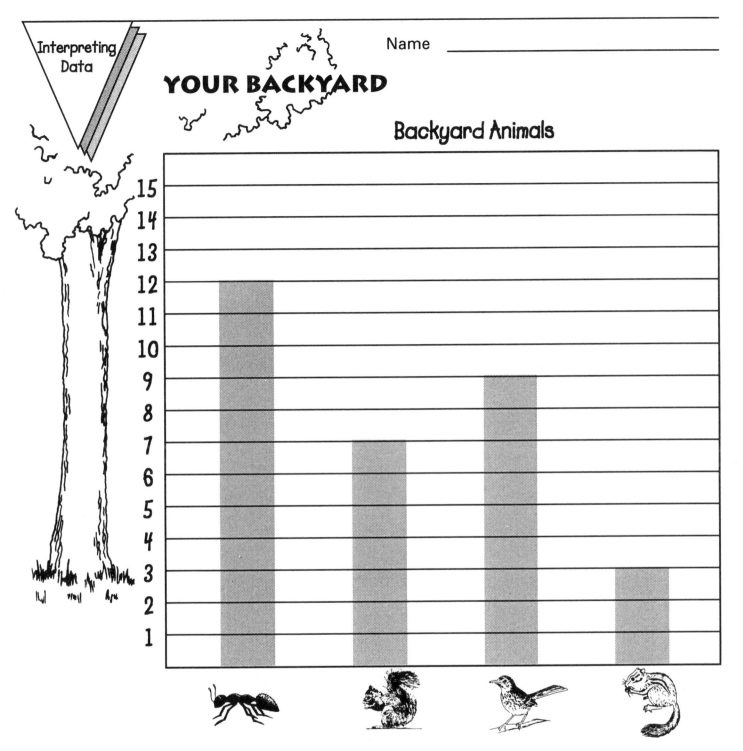

Backyard Animals

Use the graph to answer the questions below.

1. Are there more squirrels or birds?_____

2. Are there more squirrels or chipmunks?_____

3. Are there more ants or squirrels? _____

4. Are there more birds or ants?_____

Name _____

TAKE A SPIN

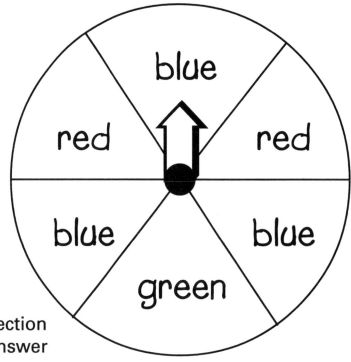

Correctly color each section of the spinner. Then answer the questions.

1. How many sections are blue? _____

2. How many sections are red? _____

3. How many sections are green? _____

4. How many sections does the spinner have altogether? _____

5. What is the probability your spinner will land on blue? *3 out of 6, or 3/6*

6. What is the probability your spinner will land on red? _____

7. What is the probability your spinner will land on green? _____

8. What is the probability your spinner will land on yellow? _____

Name _____

INSECT INFORMATION

Answer these questions.

1. If you closed your eyes and placed your finger in the box above, what kind of bug do you think your finger would probably land on?_____
   Why do you think that? _____

2. What is the probability your finger will land on a butterfly? _____

3. What is the probability your finger will land on an ant? _____

4. What is the probability your finger will land on a bee? _____

5. Which bug has the best chance of being pointed to? _____

6. Which bug has the least chance of being pointed to? _____

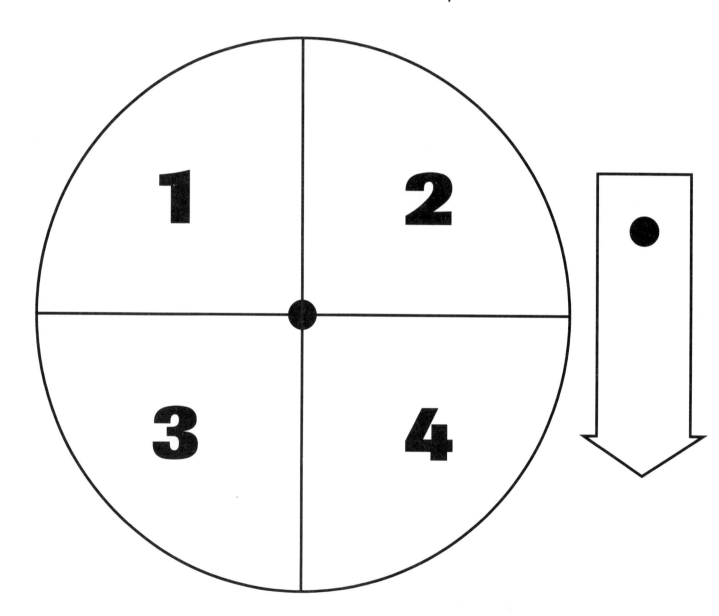

Name _____

Use with pp. 21- 23.

SPINNER FUN

To Make a Spinner

You need a brad and a piece of cardboard or tagboard and a copy of this page. Glue the patterns to the cardboard and cut them out. Pierce a hole in the arrow and in the center of the spinner. Using the brad, connect the arrow to the spinner.

Before using your spinner, predict which number you think will be spun the most and why. Record your guesses on the prediction sheet (p. 21). Then record on your tally sheet (p. 22) the number of times each number comes up.

Name _____

Use with pp. 20, 22 - 24.

SPINNER FUN (PREDICTIONS)

Before you begin, decide the total number of times the spinner will be spun. Write that number below. Then record your predictions by filling in the blanks in the Predictions section.

The spinner will be spun _____ times.

Predictions

I think the number **four** will be spun _____ times.

I think the number **three** will be spun _____ times.

I think the number **two** will be spun _____ times.

I think the number **one** will be spun _____ times.

Name _____

SPINNER FUN (TALLY SHEET) Use with pp. 20, 21, 23, 24, and 30.

Use this tally sheet to keep track of the number of spins.

1	2
3	4

Save this sheet for page 30.

SPINNER FUN (COMPARISON SHEET)

Prediction

What I predicted on page 21:

Number of **4** spins: _____

Number of **3** spins: _____

Number of **2** spins: _____

Number of **1** spins: _____

Tally Sheet Results

What my tally sheet on page 22 shows:

Number of **4** spins: _____

Number of **3** spins: _____

Number of **2** spins: _____

Number of **1** spins: _____

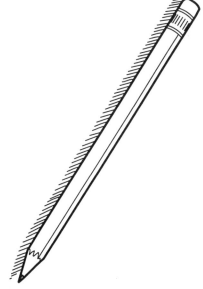

Name _____

ANOTHER SPINNER

To Make Spinner:

You need a brad and a piece of cardboard or tagboard and a copy of this page. Glue the patterns to a piece of cardboard and cut them out. Pierce a hole in the arrow and in the center of the spinner. Using the brad, connect the arrow to the spinner.

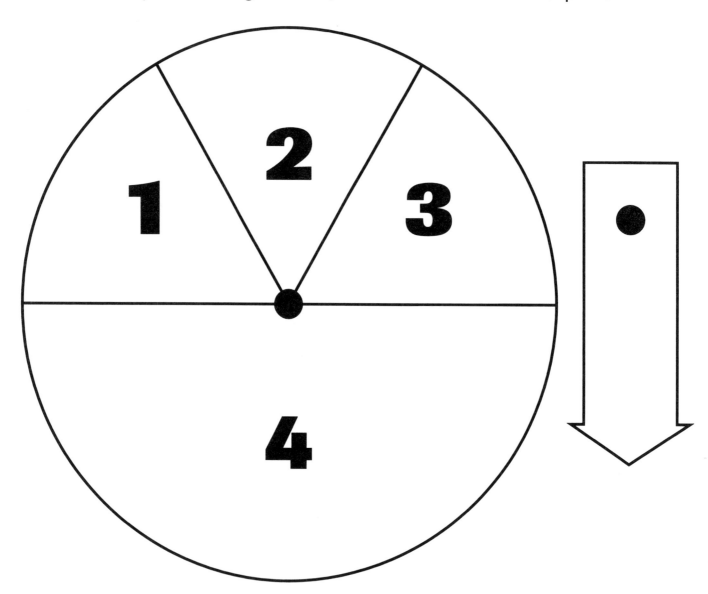

Before using your spinner, predict which number you think will be spun the most and why. Record your guesses on the prediction sheet (a copy of p. 21). Then record on the tally sheet (a copy of p. 22) the number of times each number comes up. Compare your predictions with the tally sheet results on the spinner comparison sheet (a copy of p. 23).

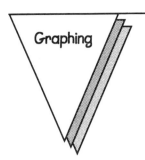

GRAPHING GAME

Working in small groups, each person takes a turn spinning and then records on his/her own graph the number he/she spun by filling in a box in that number's column. The first one to complete one column and reach the finish line wins!

1	2	3	4

Finish Line

Name _____

Use with p. 24.

ADD AND GRAPH

Working in small groups, each student spins the spinner twice, adds those two numbers together, and records the sum on his/her own graph by filling in a square in that number's column. The first one to reach the finish line wins. Example: The first spin is 1 and the second is 3, so 1 + 3 = 4. Fill in the first square under the number 4 column.

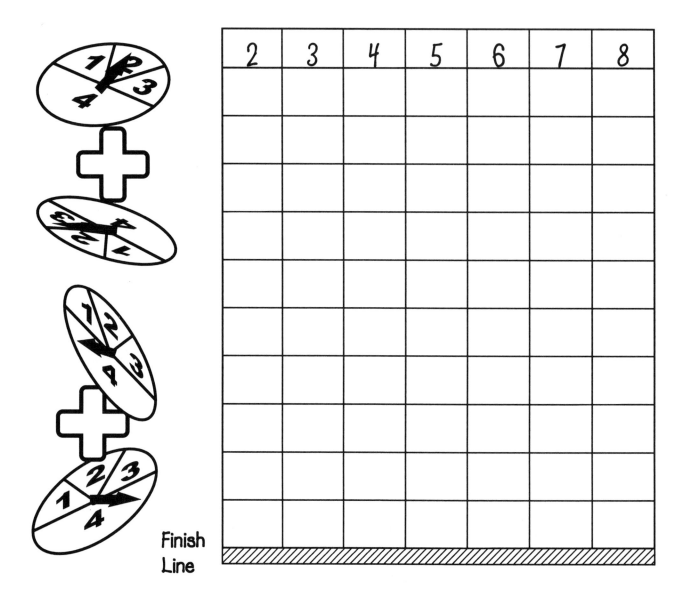

2	3	4	5	6	7	8

Finish Line

Extension Activity: Explore which sum above has the greatest number of addends. Can you predict from this which sum will most often occur?

Name _____

ANOTHER GRAPHING GAME!

Using the sum of two spins, each student fills in the boxes up to the number of the sum. With each turn, the new sum is added to the previous sum. The first one to the bottom wins! Example: Spin 1 and 3, so 1 + 3 = 4. Fill in up to box 4. Next spins are 4 and 1, so 4 + 1 = 5. Add 5 to last answer, so 5 + 4 = 9. Fill in boxes up to 9.

Player One	
2	
3	
4	
5	
6	
7	
8	
9	
10	
11	
12	
13	
14	
15	
16	
17	
18	
19	
20	
21	
22	
23	
24	
25	
26	
27	
28	
29	
30	

Player Two	
2	
3	
4	
5	
6	
7	
8	
9	
10	
11	
12	
13	
14	
15	
16	
17	
18	
19	
20	
21	
22	
23	
24	
25	
26	
27	
28	
29	
30	

27

Name _____

MAKE YOUR MIND SPIN

Look at the two spinners below and then answer the following questions.

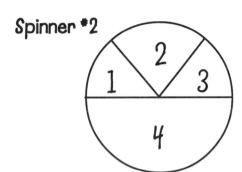

1. Which number do you think will come up the most on Spinner #2? _____
   Why do you think this? _____
   _____

2. If you were playing a game in which the highest number spun would go first,
   which spinner would you want to use? _____ Why? _____
   _____

3. If you were playing a game in which the lowest number spun would go first,
   which spinner would you want to use? _____ Why? _____
   _____

4. If you spin four times on Spinner #1, do you think it likely that all the
   numbers will come up the same amount of times? _____
   Why? _____

5. If you spin four times on Spinner #2, do you think it likely that all the
   numbers will come up the same amount of times? _____
   Why? _____

Extension Activity: Test the predictions you made above using the spinners from pages 20 and 24.

Name _____

EXPLAIN THIS, PLEASE

Use the data from the graph to
answer the questions below.

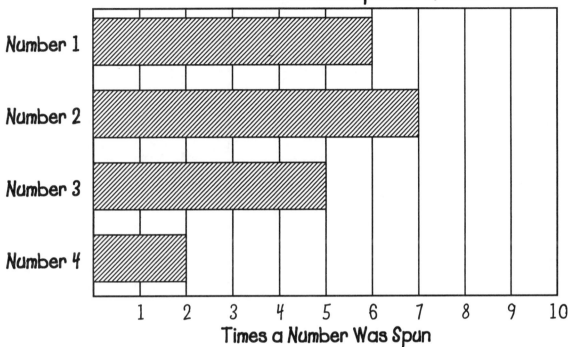

Classroom Spinner Results

1. Which number was spun the most? _____

2. Which number was spun the least? _____

3. Were any numbers spun an equal number of times? _____

4. How many times was 4 spun? _____

5. How many 2s and 4s altogether were spun? _____
   Write the number sentence. _____

6. How many 1s and 4s were spun altogether? _____
   Write the number sentence. _____

7. How many spins were there in all? _____
   Write the number sentence. _____

Name _____

GRAPHING SPINS

Using the spins recorded on a spinner tally sheet (p. 22), graph them correctly, then answer the questions below.

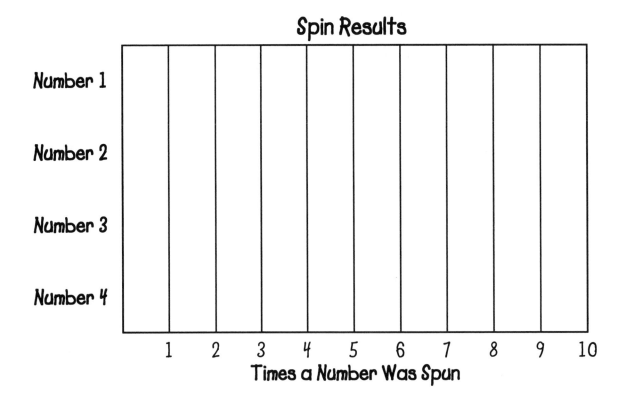

1. Which number was spun the most? _____

2. Which number was spun the least? _____

3. Were any numbers spun an equal number of times? _____

   Which ones? _____

4. How many 2s and 4s in all were spun? _____

   Write the number sentence. _____

5. How many 3s and 4s altogether were spun? _____

   Write the number sentence. _____

6. How many spins were there altogether? _____

   Write the number sentence. _____

30

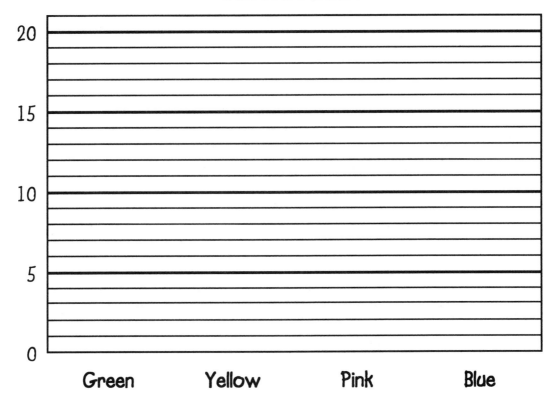

Name _____

I PREFER PINK

Correctly color the rectangles below. Then survey the students in your classroom about the color they like best of the choices below. Put a tally mark next to each person's choice.

Green _____

Yellow _____

Pink _____

Blue _____

Use the data that you have collected from your survey to complete the graph below.

Favorite Color

	Green	Yellow	Pink	Blue
20				
15				
10				
5				
0				

Name _____

SPAGHETTI OR PIZZA?

Survey each student in your classroom about his/her favorite food of the choices below. Put a tally mark next to the person's choice.

Spaghetti _____

Pizza _____

Chicken _____

Hamburger _____

Use the data you have collected from your survey to complete the graph below.

Favorite Foods

```
20 ┤
   │
15 ┤
   │
10 ┤
   │
 5 ┤
   │
 0 ┴
```

Name _____

SPORTS DATA

Use the graph to answer the questions below.

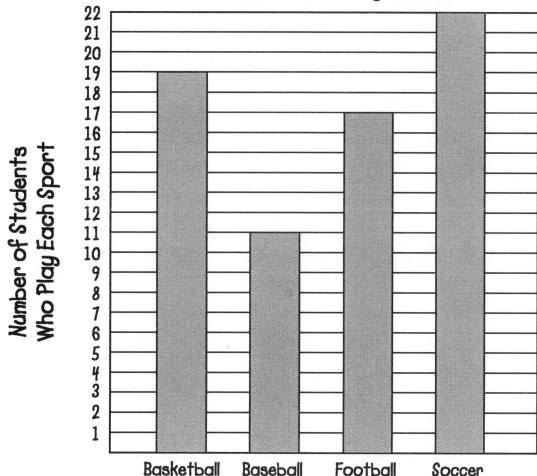

Sports Played by Third Graders at Creston Elementary School

1. Which sport is played by the greatest number of students?_____
2. Which sport is played by the least number of students?_____
3. What is played by more students, soccer or basketball?_____
4. What is played by more students, baseball or football?_____
5. What is played by more students, baseball or soccer?_____
6. What is played by more students, football or basketball?_____

Name _____

THE ONLY WAY TO TRAVEL

Graph the following data. (It was collected from two second-grade classrooms.)

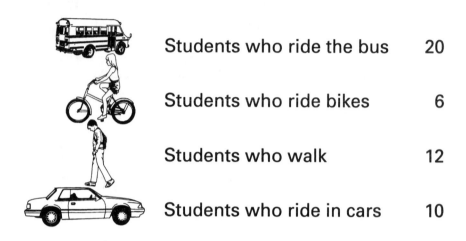

Students who ride the bus	20
Students who ride bikes	6
Students who walk	12
Students who ride in cars	10

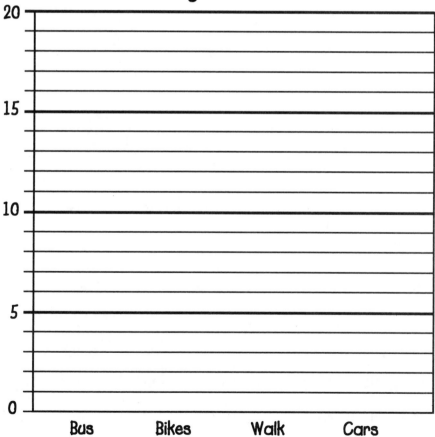

Ways to School

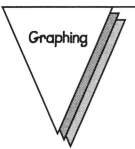

Name _____

RUN AND GRAPH IT!

Michelle loves to run! The table below shows how many miles she ran each day during one week.

Monday	2 miles
Tuesday	1 mile
Wednesday	2 miles
Thursday	2 miles
Friday	3 miles

Make a graph using the data from the table above.

Monday　　**Tuesday**　　**Wednesday**　　**Thursday**　　**Friday**

Name _____

AVERAGE AWAY

Solve the following problems.

1. How many marbles in all are there?_____

2. Three people want to share the marbles equally. How many
   would each person get?_____

1. How many baseball cards in all are there?_____

2. Two people want to share the cards evenly. How many would
   each person get?_____

Name _____

THE MEAN!

Solve the following problems.

1. Mary, Jamie, and Mike want to share their marbles equally. Mary has 12, Mike has 14, and Jamie has 10. They will combine their marbles and then divide them equally. Circle the average number each friend will have.

2. Carey, Rosa, and Terry want to share their beads when they make necklaces. Carey has 11 beads, Rosa has 9 beads, and Terry has 7 beads. They each want the same number of beads on their necklaces. Circle the average number of beads each friend will have.

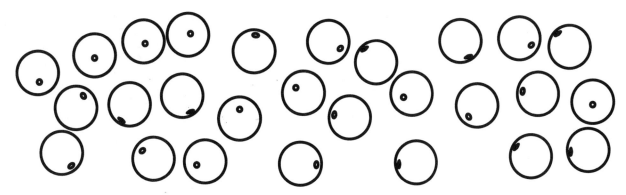

3. When John, Mark, and Fred checked their pockets, they had 24 sticks of gum altogether. If they share their gum equally, what is the average number of sticks of gum each person would have? _____

Name _____

MORE MEAN!

Solve the following problems.

1. Dave, Chris, and Jessie each have some jellybeans. Dave has 12, Chris has 15, and Jessie has 6. They want to combine their jellybeans and then divide them equally. Circle the average number each friend will have.

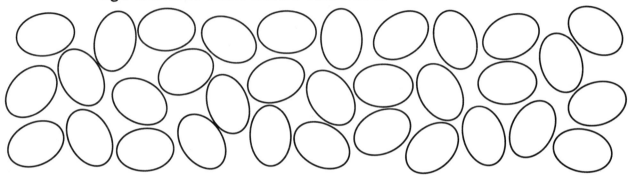

2. Susan has 5 pencils. Mary has 4 pencils. Joe has 6 pencils. They want to combine their pencils and then divide them equally. Circle the average number of pencils each friend will have.

3. John has 11 pogs, and Mike has 12 pogs. Katie has 13 pogs. They will put all their pogs together and then divide them equally. Circle the average number of pogs each friend will have.

Name _____

ABOVE AVERAGE ANSWERS

Find the **mean** of the following numbers. The first one is done for you.

1. 14, 9, 10, 2, and 5   The **average**, or **mean**, is ____8____ .

> $14 + 9 + 10 + 2 + 5 = 40$
>
> $40 \div 5 = 8$

2. 13, 12, 7, 3, and 10   The **average**, or **mean**, is _____ .

3. 8, 12, 7, 8, and 5   The **average**, or **mean**, is _____ .

4. 4, 6, 3, 7, 9, and 1   The **average**, or **mean**, is _____ .

5. 17, 3, 6, 7, and 2   The **average**, or **mean**, is _____ .

6. 9, 6, 7, and 6   The **average**, or **mean**, is _____ .

7. 8, 3, 4, 3, 6, and 0   The **average**, or **mean**, is _____ .

8. 12, 8, 6, 10, and 9   The **average**, or **mean**, is _____ .

Name _____

AROUND TOWN

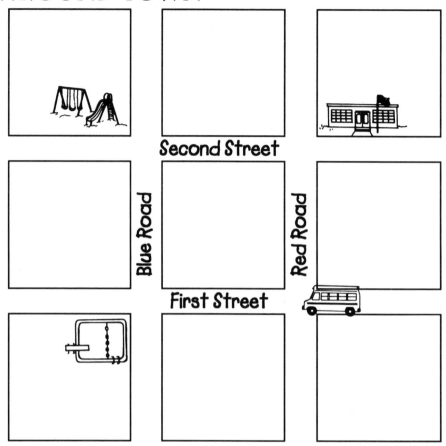

Read each question and circle the correct answer.

1. What is at the corner of First Street and Red Road?

2. What is at the corner of Second Street and Red Road?

3. What is at the corner of First Street and Blue Road?

4. What is at the corner of Second Street and Blue Road?

Name _____

TERRIFIC TRANSPORTATION

Here is how you find **A2** on the map. Go right to find **A.** Put your finger on it. Move your finger up two lines. You are at the .

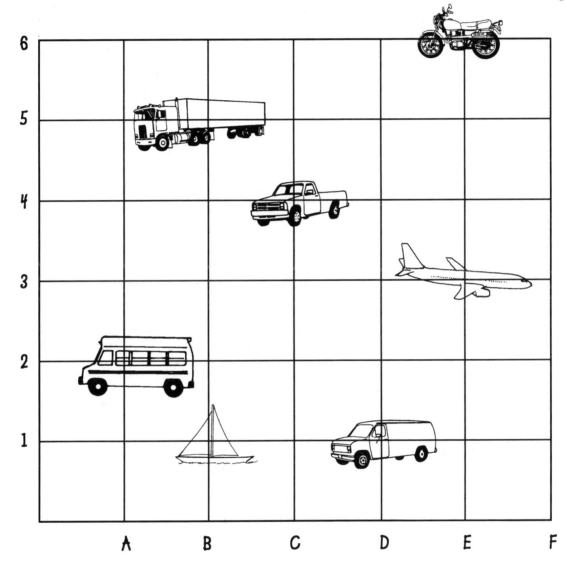

Circle the correct picture below to show what vehicle is at each point.

1. C, 4

2. D, 1

3. B, 5

4. E, 3

5. B, 1

6. E, 6

Name _____

DINOSAUR DISCOVERY

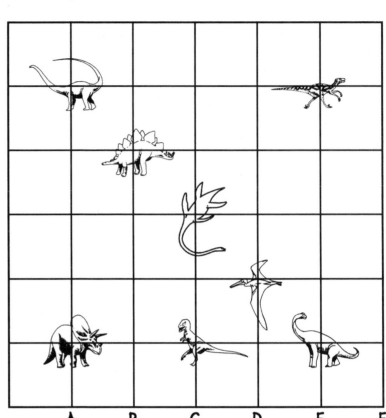

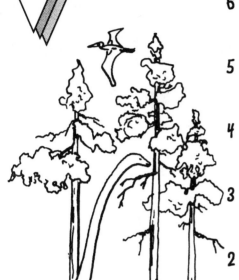

Write the name of the point where each prehistoric animal is found.

 1. _A, 1_    5. _____

 2. _____    6. _____

 3. _____    7. _____

 4. _____    8. _____

Name _____

LET'S GO, TEAM!

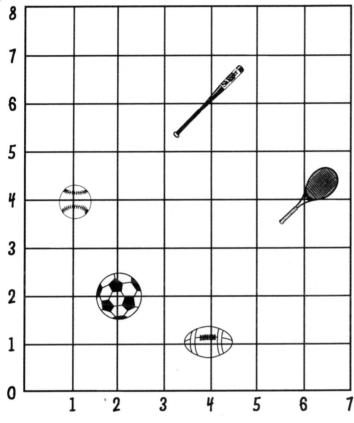

Circle the correct answer for each ordered pair.

1. What is at (2, 2)?

2. What is at (4, 1)?

3. What is at (6, 4)?

4. What is at (1, 4)?

5. What is at (4, 6)?

Name _____

A WALK IN THE ZOO

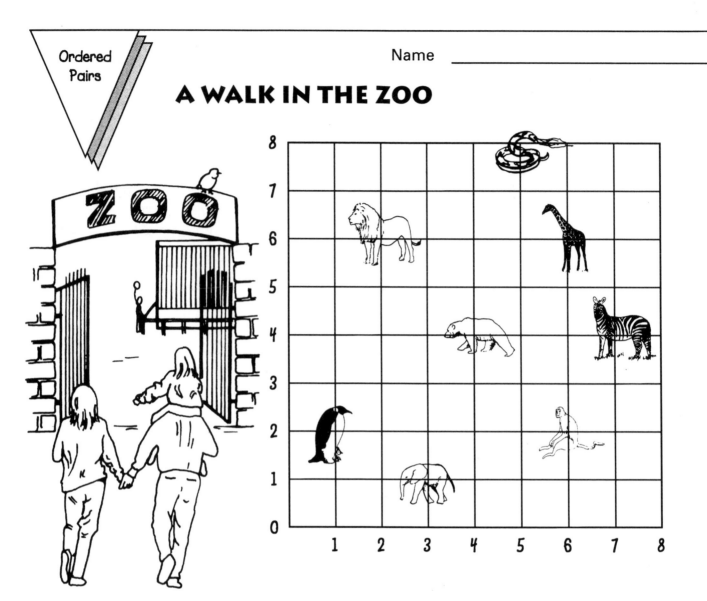

Answer the following questions by writing the correct ordered pair.

1. Where is the lion? _____

2. Where is the bear? _____

3. Where is the giraffe? _____

4. Where is the monkey? _____

5. Where is the penguin? _____

6. Where is the snake? _____

7. Where is the zebra? _____

8. Where is the elephant? _____

Name _____

SPACE TRAVEL

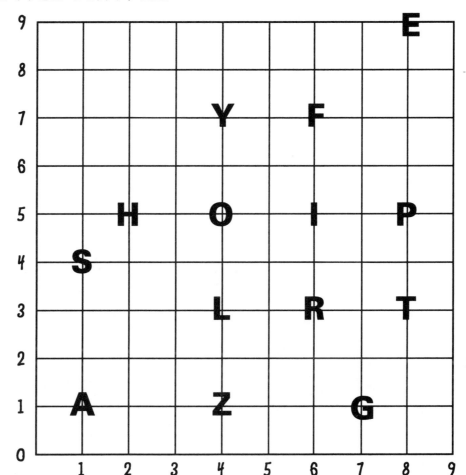

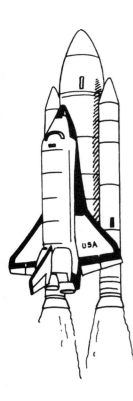

Solve the riddle below by writing the correct letter next to each ordered pair.

1. (4, 3) _____
2. (6, 5) _____
3. (7, 1) _____
4. (2, 5) _____
5. (8, 3) _____

6. (4, 7) _____
7. (8, 9) _____
8. (1, 1) _____
9. (6, 3) _____
10. (1, 4) _____

Riddle: How do we measure distance to and between stars?

Read down. The riddle answer is _____.

45

ANSWER KEY

Not all pages have
an answer key.

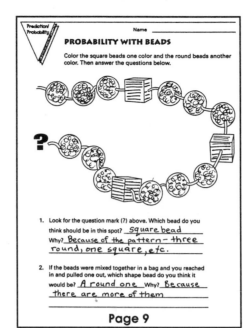

Name _____

PROBABILITY WITH BEADS

Color the square beads one color and the round beads another color. Then answer the questions below.

1. Look for the question mark (?) above. Which bead do you think should be in this spot? _square bead_ Why? _Because of the pattern - three round, one square, etc._

2. If the beads were mixed together in a bag and you reached in and pulled one out, which shape bead do you think it would be? _A round one_ Why? _Because there are more of them_

Page 9

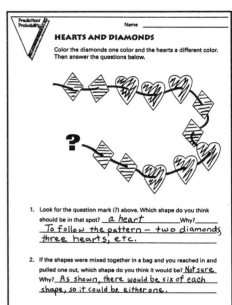

Name _____

HEARTS AND DIAMONDS

Color the diamonds one color and the hearts a different color. Then answer the questions below.

1. Look for the question mark (?) above. Which shape do you think should be in that spot? _a heart_ Why? _To follow the pattern - two diamonds, three hearts, etc._

2. If the shapes were mixed together in a bag and you reached in and pulled one out, which shape do you think it would be? _Not sure_ Why? _As shown, there would be six of each shape, so it could be either one._

Page 10

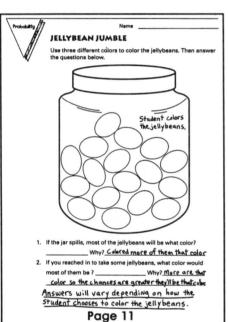

Name _____

JELLYBEAN JUMBLE

Use three different colors to color the jellybeans. Then answer the questions below.

Student colors the jellybeans.

1. If the jar spills, most of the jellybeans will be what color? _____ Why? _Colored more of them that color_

2. If you reached in to take some jellybeans, what color would most of them be? _____ Why? _More are that color so the chances are greater they'll be that color_ _Answers will vary depending on how the student chooses to color the jellybeans._

Page 11

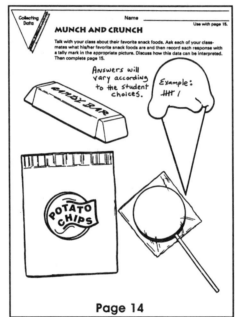

Name _____   Use with page 15.

MUNCH AND CRUNCH

Talk with your class about their favorite snack foods. Ask each of your classmates what his/her favorite snack foods are and then record each response with a tally mark in the appropriate picture. Discuss how this data can be interpreted. Then complete page 15.

Answers will vary according to the student choices.

Example: HHH I

Page 14

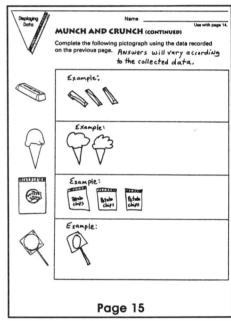

Name _____   Use with page 14.

MUNCH AND CRUNCH (CONTINUED)

Complete the following pictograph using the data recorded on the previous page. _Answers will vary according to the collected data._

Example:

Example:

Example:

Example:

Page 15

Name _____

SUNNY SKIES

The pictures show the weather for one month. Look at the number of sunny, cloudy, and rainy days there were.

Create a pictograph using the data above.

Weather for One Month

Number of Days

Page 16

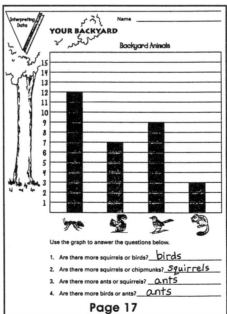

Name _____

YOUR BACKYARD

Backyard Animals

Use the graph to answer the questions below.

1. Are there more squirrels or birds? _birds_
2. Are there more squirrels or chipmunks? _squirrels_
3. Are there more ants or squirrels? _ants_
4. Are there more birds or ants? _ants_

Page 17

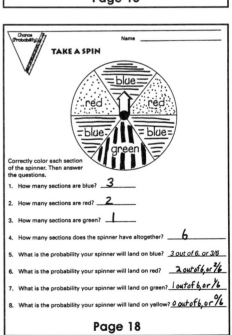

Name _____

TAKE A SPIN

Correctly color each section of the spinner. Then answer the questions.

1. How many sections are blue? _3_
2. How many sections are red? _2_
3. How many sections are green? _1_
4. How many sections does the spinner have altogether? _6_
5. What is the probability your spinner will land on blue? _3 out of 6, or 3/6_
6. What is the probability your spinner will land on red? _2 out of 6, or 2/6_
7. What is the probability your spinner will land on green? _1 out of 6, or 1/6_
8. What is the probability your spinner will land on yellow? _0 out of 6, or 0/6_

Page 18

Page 19

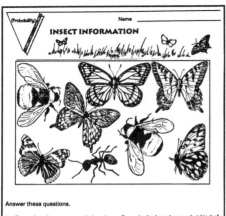

(Probability)

INSECT INFORMATION

Answer these questions.

1. If you closed your eyes and placed your finger in the box above, what kind of bug do you think your finger would probably land on? **a butterfly**
   Why do you think that? **Because there are more butterflies**
2. What is the probability your finger will land on a butterfly? **5 out of 8, or 5/8**
3. What is the probability your finger will land on an ant? **1 out of 8, or 1/8**
4. What is the probability your finger will land on a bee? **2 out of 8, or 3/8**
5. Which bug has the best chance of being pointed to? **a butterfly**
6. Which bug has the least chance of being pointed to? **the ant**

Page 19

Page 21

Prediction

SPINNER FUN (PREDICTIONS)

Before you begin, decide the total number of times the spinner will be spun. Write that number below. Then record your predictions by filling in the blanks in the Predictions section.

The spinner will be spun _____ times.

Answers will vary, but predictions should add up to the total above.

Predictions

I think the number **four** will be spun _____ times.

I think the number **three** will be spun _____ times.

I think the number **two** will be spun _____ times.

I think the number **one** will be spun _____ times.

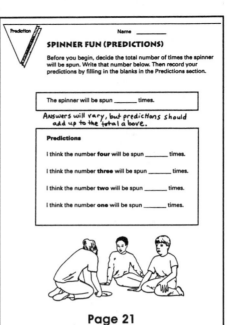

Page 21

Page 28

Probability

MAKE YOUR MIND SPIN

Look at the two spinners below and then answer the following questions.

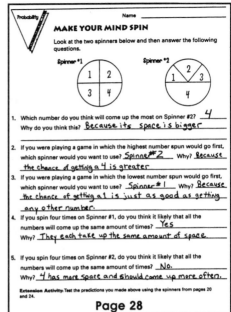

Spinner #1 — 1 2 / 3 4

Spinner #2 — 1 2 / 3 / 4

1. Which number do you think will come up the most on Spinner #2? **4**
   Why do you think this? **Because its space is bigger**
2. If you were playing a game in which the highest number spun would go first, which spinner would you want to use? **Spinner #2** Why? **Because the chance of getting a 4 is greater**
3. If you were playing a game in which the lowest number spun would go first, which spinner would you want to use? **Spinner #1** Why? **Because the chance of getting a 1 is just as good as getting any other number.**
4. If you spin four times on Spinner #1, do you think it likely that all the numbers will come up the same amount of times? **Yes**
   Why? **They each take up the same amount of space.**
5. If you spin four times on Spinner #2, do you think it likely that all the numbers will come up the same amount of times? **No.**
   Why? **4 has more space and should come up more often.**

Extension Activity: Test the predictions you made above using the spinners from pages 20 and 24.

Page 28

Page 29

Interpreting Data

EXPLAIN THIS, PLEASE

Use the data from the graph to answer the questions below.

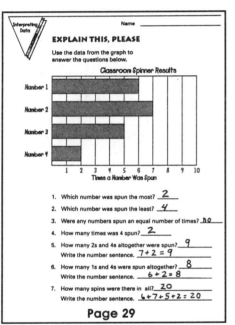

Classroom Spinner Results

1. Which number was spun the most? **2**
2. Which number was spun the least? **4**
3. Were any numbers spun an equal number of times? **no**
4. How many times was 4 spun? **2**
5. How many 2s and 4s altogether were spun? **9**
   Write the number sentence. **7 + 2 = 9**
6. How many 1s and 4s were spun altogether? **8**
   Write the number sentence. **6 + 2 = 8**
7. How many spins were there in all? **20**
   Write the number sentence. **6 + 7 + 5 + 2 = 20**

Page 29

Page 31

Surveying/Graphing

I PREFER PINK

Correctly color the rectangles below. Then survey the students in your classroom about the color they like best of the choices below. Put a tally mark next to each person's choice.

Answers will vary

(Green) Green **Example: HH**
(Yellow) Yellow
(Pink) Pink
(Blue) Blue

Use the data that you have collected from your survey to complete the graph below.

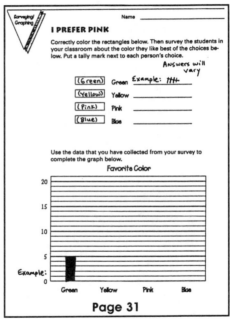

Favorite Color

Page 31

Page 33

Interpreting Data

SPORTS DATA

Use the graph to answer the questions below.

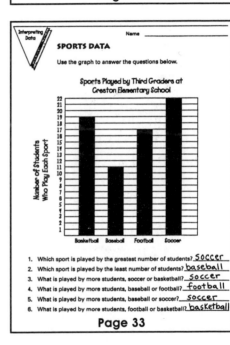

Sports Played by Third Graders at Creston Elementary School

1. Which sport is played by the greatest number of students? **soccer**
2. Which sport is played by the least number of students? **baseball**
3. What is played by more students, soccer or basketball? **soccer**
4. What is played by more students, baseball or football? **football**
5. What is played by more students, baseball or soccer? **soccer**
6. What is played by more students, football or basketball? **basketball**

Page 33

Page 34

Graphing

THE ONLY WAY TO TRAVEL

Graph the following data. (It was collected from two second-grade classrooms.)

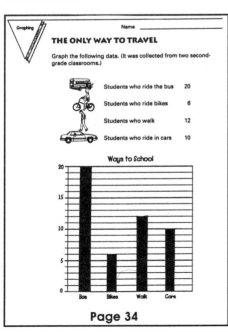

Students who ride the bus — 20
Students who ride bikes — 6
Students who walk — 12
Students who ride in cars — 10

Ways to School

Page 34

Page 35

Graphing

RUN AND GRAPH IT!

Michelle loves to run! The table below shows how many miles she ran each day during one week.

Monday	2 miles
Tuesday	1 mile
Wednesday	2 miles
Thursday	2 miles
Friday	3 miles

Make a graph using the data from the table above. **Graphs may vary.**

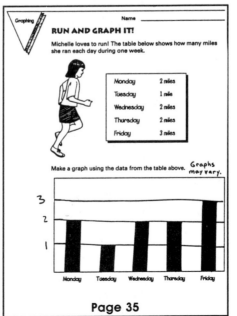

Page 35

Page 36

Finding the Average (the Mean)

AVERAGE AWAY

Solve the following problems.

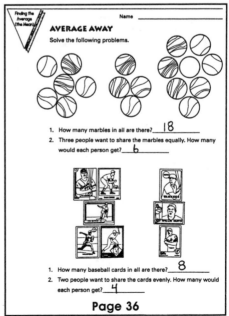

1. How many marbles in all are there? **18**
2. Three people want to share the marbles equally. How many would each person get? **6**

1. How many baseball cards in all are there? **8**
2. Two people want to share the cards evenly. How many would each person get? **4**

Page 36

© Instructional Fair • TS Denison   47   IF5118 *Probabilities, Statistics, & Graphing—Primary*

THE MEAN!

Name _____

Solve the following problems.

1. Mary, Jamie, and Mike want to share their marbles equally. Mary has 12, Mike has 14, and Jamie has 10. They will combine their marbles and then divide them equally. Circle the average number each friend will have.

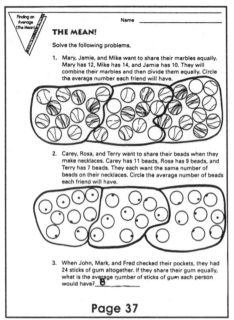

2. Carey, Rosa, and Terry want to share their beads when they make necklaces. Carey has 11 beads, Rosa has 9 beads, and Terry has 7 beads. They each want the same number of beads on their necklaces. Circle the average number of beads each friend will have.

3. When John, Mark, and Fred checked their pockets, they had 24 sticks of gum altogether. If they share their gum equally, what is the average number of sticks of gum each person would have? **8**

Page 37

MORE MEAN!

Name _____

Solve the following problems.

1. Dave, Chris, and Jessie each have some jellybeans. Dave has 12, Chris has 15, and Jessie has 6. They want to combine their jellybeans and then divide them equally. Circle the average number each friend will have.

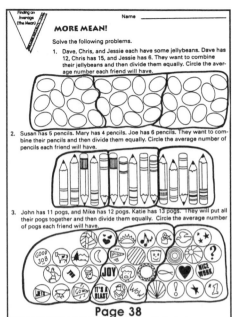

2. Susan has 5 pencils. Mary has 4 pencils. Joe has 6 pencils. They want to combine their pencils and then divide them equally. Circle the average number of pencils each friend will have.

3. John has 11 pogs, and Mike has 12 pogs. Katie has 13 pogs. They will put all their pogs together and then divide them equally. Circle the average number of pogs each friend will have.

Page 38

ABOVE AVERAGE ANSWERS

Name _____

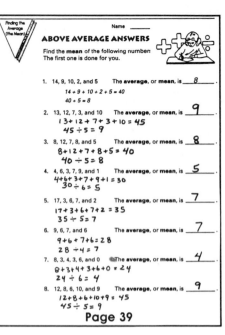

Find the **mean** of the following number. The first one is done for you.

1. 14, 9, 10, 2, and 5   The **average**, or **mean**, is ___8___
   $14 + 9 + 10 + 2 + 5 = 40$
   $40 \div 5 = 8$

2. 13, 12, 7, 3, and 10   The **average**, or **mean**, is ___9___
   $13 + 12 + 7 + 3 + 10 = 45$
   $45 \div 5 = 9$

3. 8, 12, 7, 8, and 5   The **average**, or **mean**, is ___8___
   $8 + 12 + 7 + 8 + 5 = 40$
   $40 \div 5 = 8$

4. 4, 6, 3, 7, 9, and 1   The **average**, or **mean**, is ___5___
   $4 + 6 + 3 + 7 + 9 + 1 = 30$
   $30 \div 6 = 5$

5. 17, 3, 6, 7, and 2   The **average**, or **mean**, is ___7___
   $17 + 3 + 6 + 7 + 2 = 35$
   $35 \div 5 = 7$

6. 9, 6, 7, and 6   The **average**, or **mean**, is ___7___
   $9 + 6 + 7 + 6 = 28$
   $28 \div 4 = 7$

7. 8, 3, 4, 3, 6, and 0   The **average**, or **mean**, is ___4___
   $8 + 3 + 4 + 3 + 6 + 0 = 24$
   $24 \div 6 = 4$

8. 12, 8, 6, 10, and 9   The **average**, or **mean**, is ___9___
   $12 + 8 + 6 + 10 + 9 = 45$
   $45 \div 5 = 9$

Page 39

AROUND TOWN

Name _____

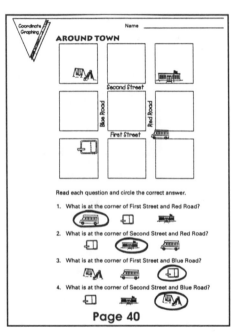

Read each question and circle the correct answer.

1. What is at the corner of First Street and Red Road?

2. What is at the corner of Second Street and Red Road?

3. What is at the corner of First Street and Blue Road?

4. What is at the corner of Second Street and Blue Road?

Page 40

TERRIFIC TRANSPORTATION

Name _____

Here is how you find **A2** on the map. Go right to find **A**. Put your finger on it. Move your finger up two lines. You are at the 🚌.

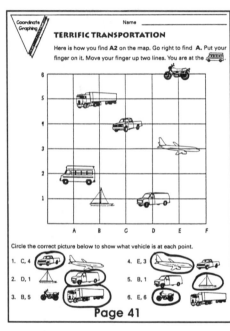

Circle the correct picture below to show what vehicle is at each point.

1. C, 4
2. D, 1
3. B, 5
4. E, 3
5. B, 1
6. E, 6

Page 41

DINOSAUR DISCOVERY

Name _____

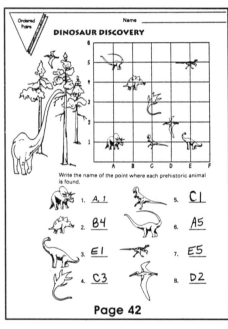

Write the name of the point where each prehistoric animal is found.

1. _A, 1_
2. _B4_
3. _E1_
4. _C3_
5. _C1_
6. _A5_
7. _E5_
8. _D2_

Page 42

LET'S GO, TEAM!

Name _____

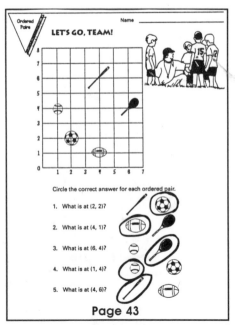

Circle the correct answer for each ordered pair.

1. What is at (2, 2)?
2. What is at (4, 1)?
3. What is at (6, 4)?
4. What is at (1, 4)?
5. What is at (4, 6)?

Page 43

A WALK IN THE ZOO

Name _____

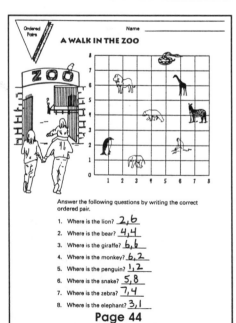

Answer the following questions by writing the correct ordered pair.

1. Where is the lion? _2,6_
2. Where is the bear? _4,4_
3. Where is the giraffe? _6,6_
4. Where is the monkey? _6,2_
5. Where is the penguin? _1,2_
6. Where is the snake? _5,8_
7. Where is the zebra? _7,4_
8. Where is the elephant? _3,1_

Page 44

SPACE TRAVEL

Name _____

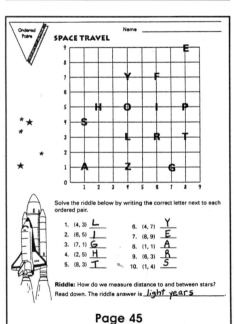

Solve the riddle below by writing the correct letter next to each ordered pair.

1. (4, 3) _L_
2. (6, 5) _I_
3. (7, 1) _G_
4. (2, 5) _H_
5. (8, 3) _T_
6. (4, 7) _Y_
7. (8, 9) _E_
8. (1, 1) _A_
9. (6, 3) _R_
10. (1, 4) _S_

Riddle: How do we measure distance to and between stars?
Read down. The riddle answer is _light years_

Page 45
